Study and Activity Guide

A companion for

Connections Remembered,

African Origins of Humanity and Civilization:

The Impact of Historical Memory on Black Identity

By

Lindiwe S. Lester and Sondai K. Lester

P.S.E. Institute, 2021

Connections Remembered: The African Origins of Humanity and Civilization, Study and Activity Guide

ISBN number: 978-1-7344826-1-4

Library of Congress Cataloguing-in-Publication Data

Lester, Lindiwe Stovall and Lester, Sondai Kibwe

Connections Remembered: African Origins of Humanity and Civilization, The Impact of Historical Memory on Black Identity, Study and Activity Guide

1. African History
2. Rites of Passage
3. African American Child Development
4. African-Centered Education
5. African American Education
6. African American History

CONTENTS

I. Introduction to the Study Guide

II.   Study Activities and Worksheets

Thank you for reading and joining this journey to reclaim healthy Black identity.

West African Adinkra symbol, the Sankofa bird
It is not wrong to go back for that which you have
forgotten

1. Introduction to the Study Guide

for Connections Remembered, The African Origins of Humanity and Civilization

"The greatest weapon in the hands of the oppressor is the mind of the oppressed."

Steve Biko (South Africa, 1946-1977)

The capacity of a people, especially an oppressed group of people, to function together productively is dependent upon the nature of their historical consciousness. Each Black person's level of awareness about who *they* are and who *we* have been within the flow and evolution of humanity impacts all Black people today.

Both children and adults of African descent have been subjected to an educational system which has largely disconnected us from the glories of our African past. That separation has been the source of a severe memory loss – a form of social amnesia that produces in us a distorted historical consciousness and a self-destructive collective identity. Not knowing who we really are, we have become, in our own minds, who our oppressor claims we are.

This study and activity guide is a companion for **Connections Remembered, The African Origins and Humanity and Civilization.** It was developed to help study participants ascribe greater meaning from the events, symbols, facts and artifacts of our history and be transformed by the knowledge of who *they* and *we* really are. May we reclaim our minds, making them weapons in our struggle for self-determination.

Purpose of the Study Guide

The aim of this study guide, a complement to **Connections Remembered**, is two-fold:

1. It offers support and a pathway for individuals to personally probe more deeply into the content of **Connections Remembered** and its impact on their own identity, and

2. It provides the educational leader a foundation to put the included activities to use and develop other meaningful activities in accordance with the learners' age levels and backgrounds.

The included activities and suggestions all have 21st Century social and political realities as their backdrop.

Who Should Use It?

This study/activity guide audience includes **anyone interested in deepening their own or others' study of Black history** and the historical foundations of Black identity. The guide is suitable for learning group leaders of adult study groups, families, rites of passage programs, and home schoolers, along with classroom teachers and college educators.

The activities are designed for use with teenagers and adults. It is possible that adults can alter the activities for work with younger ages.

The Intersection of Content and Process for Learning

Fundamental to the information and activities in this study guide are the basic components of a *learning process approach* to making meaning of the content of **Connections Remembered**. In that vein, the study guide was developed based on recognizing that the acquisition of knowledge embodies both *objective content and the process* for internalizing and making meaning of that content. The book, **Connections Remembered**, in this case is the **content**. This study guide is meant to serve as a **process** tool.

Learning is limited when you separate the content from process. Dr. Donald Treffinger, president of the Center for Creative Learning Inc., aptly states,

It is not just about content anymore, but rather process and content as equal players. Content is important because you have to think creatively about something; but there are also process skills and tools for thinking creatively, critically, and solving problems that students need to learn explicitly and intentionally.[1] p.7

The study guide seeks to move the individual from focusing passively on memorizing the content (what you know) to deeply contemplating *what you think about* what you know.

Currently learning is primarily, if not solely, content centered. Far too often, the learning process can be likened to what Paulo Freire defines as the **banking concept of education**, a format for education around the world especially for those who are oppressed. In defining this form of education, the esteemed philosopher and educator said,

The teacher as narrator leads the students to memorize mechanically the narrated content. Worse yet, it turns them into containers, into receptacles to be filled by the teacher. The more completely he fills the receptacles, the better a teacher he/she is. The more meekly the receptacles permit themselves to be filled, the better students they are. Education becomes an act of depositing, in which the students are the depositories, and the teacher is the depositor.[2] p. 58

A child sits in the classroom as an empty vessel patiently waiting for the teacher to make deposits of the required content into their head to be memorized for the test. In Freire's

---

[1] Cited in Green, Nancy. More than cupcakes: Supporting your child's creative potential. *Parenting for High Potential*, June 2009.
[2] Freire, Paulo. 1974. *Pedagogy of the oppressed.*

"banking" model of education, the student is a passive participant in their own education waiting to be told by the teacher what to think and subsequently what to do. It is that kind of teaching that leads the student to a quiet adaptation to and acceptance of the status quo. It is precisely that kind of teaching that cripples critical thinking and creativity while undermining any inclination to question and challenge the world as it exists.

The process used in this study guide enables learners to become active participants in their learning and can lead to raising some fundamental questions to deepen learning: *What if? What new questions does this raise? What new ideas come to mind? What does it mean for me personally (identity)? What must I do now?* When process is added to content the learner takes more control of their learning.

Fostering Critical 21st Century Competencies

Another focus of the study guide's process is the 21ˢᵗ Century educational competencies necessary to function productively in the modern technological information age. Tony Wagner in *The Global Achievement Gap* writes this about the current educational challenge:

> *We are confronted by exponential increases of readily available information, new technologies that are constantly changing, and more complex societal challenges. Thus, work, learning, and citizenship in the twenty-first century demand that we know how to think—to reason, analyze, weigh evidence, problem-solve, and to communicate effectively. These are no longer skills that only the elites in a society must master; they are essential survival skills for all of us. While Johnny, and Juan and Leticia are learning how to read, at least at a basic level, they are not learning how to think or care about what they read; nor are they learning to clearly communicate orally or in writing. p. xxiii*

This study guide emphasizes four of these essential survival competencies, and also includes self-reflection. As such, **five competencies are being cultivated through the included activities, and are:**

1. **Question formulation**
2. **Critical thinking**
3. **Creativity/innovation**
4. **Collaborative analysis and problem solving**
5. **Self-reflection/metacognition (thinking about your thinking)**

The strategies embedded in the study guide can provide a basis for the learner to build historical and cultural fluency, come to see the world more clearly, and engage in behaviors that can transform that world.

How the Study Guide Is Structured

The study guide is aligned with ***Connections Remembered's*** related Preface and eight sections. Each section of this study guide includes:

- Suggested study group objective(s)
- A snapshot of the book's section and its main points
- Key terms and people
- A quotation related to the content
- Three to five activity options. A few activities are expansions of the activities included in the book. Some activities foster content recall and others engage participants in probing deeper for meaning.
- Reproducible worksheets, handouts, and charts

Each section includes opportunities for learners to:

- Brainstorm questions
- Reflect and apply learning to real life
- Pose new questions at the close of each section

Preparation For the Study/Process Leader

You have an exciting and multi-faceted role. While study groups do not typically require loads of preparation beyond scheduling logistics, assigning readings, and having a few questions, you may want to think about your role as the process leader in multiple ways. To the right is a simple graphic that suggests the common roles a study leader assumes, sometime intuitively, but why not be intentionally prepared to lead dynamic,

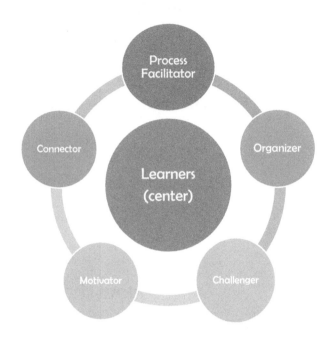

transformational sessions? *Notice the **learners** are at the center of the graphic because the learning really belongs to them, not the learning leader.*

Five Roles	Description
1. Process Facilitator	Guide the session in a way designed for the group to achieve its goals, deepen and apply knowledge, while maintaining momentum, focus and meaningful, respectful relationships.
2. Organizer	Handling the logistics of the sessions, such as place, time, preparation, etc. This can also be assigned to someone else.
3. Connector	Facilitate in such a way as to support learners in connecting themes to their lives, to other concepts, etc. And, just as important, connect learners with each other—their experiences, their knowledge, their values, to create a sense of community.
4. Motivator	To pay attention to interest and level of engagement and take actions to keep the sessions meaningful; to foster full participation of those who have varying degrees of assertiveness.
5. Challenger	To use great questions to challenge the learners to think more deeply, to open their thinking to new perspectives, to trust their thoughts, etc.

Questions you might ask yourself:

Am I knowledgeable of the content? Have I come up with a few clear and thought-provoking questions to get the group's mental wheels turning? Am I helping the group make meaning from the content? Am I connecting the dots—between the learners' input and the book's content? Am I adaptable in my own thinking, open to new insights from the participants? Do I motivate and challenge the group to think deeper about the content beyond memorization? Do I inspire them to believe in their own thoughts and potential? Do the sessions I lead leave participants more interested and curious? Do I handle the study group session in a way that intentionally includes various perspectives?

Four Functions for the Study/Process Leader

To effectively use the study guide, we suggest study leaders not only prompt the group to recall the information, but the leader should also prepare for four functions that transform the study group dynamics and learning from average to great. These functions require the study leader to:

1. Guide the learning group by using *more questions and less telling*
2. Encourage participants to generate and probe their own questions (page 13)
3. Lead and facilitate groups for impact (see pages 14-16)
4. Make use of the included activities (see checklist on **Page 17**)

Here's a bit about each of these four functions that might support the study leader role.

1. Guide the learning group by using more questions and less telling

Asking questions is a far more powerful tool for learning than telling or lecturing a group endlessly. Yet it requires we re-set our minds about what it means to teach and guide learning. Read the following quote and reflect on it a moment.

"The usefulness of the knowledge we acquire and the effectiveness of the actions we take depend on the quality of the questions we ask. Questions open the door to dialogue and discovery. They are an invitation to creativity and breakthrough thinking. Questions can lead to movement and action on key issues; by generating creative insights, they can ignite change." **The Art of Powerful Questions**, *Vogt, Brown and Isaacs, pg. 1*

 **My Reflection:** What might this mean for my current style of leading learning groups?

Posing good questions rather than telling participants what to know and think has many benefits: fosters insight, motivates fresh thinking/creativity, and challenges outdated viewpoints. *Good questions generate energy and lead to deeper meaning.*

When we are trying to gain greater insight, use open-ended powerful questions. They are neither *leading* (phrased to suggest a pre-determined answer) nor closed-ended (requiring only a Yes, No, an either/or response or a few words). (Closed-ended questions have a place, especially to recall important facts.) **More powerful questions ask how and why.**

A few things to consider as both you and the participants learn the art of powerful inquiry:

- Practice creating and using questions that open the group's thinking. (some examples are in the **sample question bank** at the end of this section)
- Get familiar with the **question hierarchy pyramid** on the next page (a popular tool for fostering critical thinking).
- Ask questions that help learners make connections from the content to real-life.
- Avoid the temptation to answer when the group is struggling. Remember the purpose is to get them to think more deeply, explore new possibilities, and grow their confidence in wrestling with ideas and testing their assumptions.

3. Encourage participants to generate their own questions

"Society tends to make a pedagogical mistake by emphasizing the answering and not asking of questions." —Robert Sternberg

While the study leader should be skilled at posing good questions to ignite the learners' thinking, a balance should be created that ensures a number of the questions used in the study group are formulated by the learners themselves.

Here are some ways to help learners create their own questions:

1. The study leader **models** asking good questions, and learners may begin to adopt that practice.

2. The study leader **invites** learners' questions throughout the sessions; at the beginning and the end are great places to encourage creating such questions. Here is how that might look:

   a. At the beginning of the session, have the group brainstorm a list of as many questions as they can related to the material. (During brainstorming, all ideas are accepted without judgment; just make a list. If

Question Hierarchy Pyramid

Most people rank the "question starter" words from more to less powerful as indicated below.

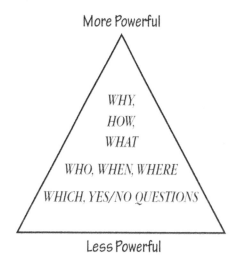

More Powerful

WHY, HOW, WHAT
WHO, WHEN, WHERE
WHICH, YES/NO QUESTIONS

Less Powerful

By using the words toward the top of the question pyramid, you can make many questions more powerful. For example, consider the following:

- Are you satisfied belonging to the study group?
- *When* are you most satisfied belonging to the group?
- *What* is it that brings the most satisfaction to you as a member of the study group?
- *Why* might it be that belonging to the group fluctuates between very satisfying to just ok?
- *How* can we make this a consistently great experience for you as a study group member?

If you notice, as you move from the simple Yes/No question at the beginning toward the Why and How questions at the end, you'll probably observe that the latter questions tend to stimulate reflection and deeper conversation.

Adapted from *The Art of Powerful Questions* by Eric Vogel

question).

 b. Next, have the group prioritize the questions they would like to have answered. Narrow the list further by selecting 3-4 most important questions. Ask the group to clarify "why" these are the most important.

 c. At the end of the study sessions, you might ask: *What did you discover related to the questions we started with? What new questions did our conversation raise for you? What further research, if any, do we need to do as a result of these conversations?* (Note: The final activity for each section of the study guide has this process included.)

3. To help learners create quality questions, refer them to the **question hierarchy pyramid on page 13**.

4. Provide opportunities for student-led discussions centered around questions generated by both students and study leader.

3. Lead and facilitate groups for impact

Facilitation means: to provide guidance to a group that *makes it easy* for them to own and take responsibility for making good decisions and achieving its goals.

A facilitator's value lies in 1) helping a group define its needs and goals related to the session, 2) providing processes (including methods and tools) to engage the participants, and 3) using skills to ensure good group dynamics so relationships are maintained, and energy is sustained. For the most part, facilitators play an objective role that allows each perspective to be considered and valued. On rare occasions, the facilitator shares his or her own thoughts because they believe it will help the group with its process.

12 Basic Facilitation Tips for Study Leaders

☑ Know your role, which is to focus on the group's process	☑ Summarize the ideas expressed by the group	☑ Remain mostly neutral
☑ Help the group establish norms for how they interact, then help reinforce them	☑ Keep the group on track	☑ Pay attention to the group's energy
☑ Talk less, listen more	☑ Try different ways to garner participation (e.g., brainstorming, round robins, polling, breakouts)	☑ Try to include everyone, "share the air"
☑ Help the group learn from each other	☑ Value everyone's input	☑ Be willing to let things emerge, adjusting the process as needed

Some other common facilitation considerations:

1. Remember, learning is best when the learners are engaged. So, ensure it's mostly the participants talking rather than you. Try to keep your speaking time to opening the session, clarifying the purpose, summarizing as needed, keeping the group focused, transitioning, asking for process feedback, and closing the session.

2. Ask the group to establish 3 -5 simple guidelines/ground rules for the study group to ensure it works well for everyone.

3. Provide opportunities for the learners to interact, share and develop ideas, and form conclusions collaboratively, rather than telling them the conclusions to reach.

4. Spend most of your time developing and asking good questions.

5. Assume the participants each bring some level of knowledge, based on their own experiences and background. So, create opportunities to integrate their knowledge, making it a shared learning experience. (*Examples: Does anyone have experiences related to our topic? What do you already know about this?, etc.*)

Sample Question Bank

(questions are more "powerful" [probe deeper] as you move from the first to the last column)

Which, Who, When & Where (closed questions)	What	Why & How
When did this happen?	What do you want to gain from this?	Why? (followed by "are there any other possibilities?")
What time do we start and end?	What impact do events have on your/their self-worth and identity?	Why is so much of the Black historical experience excluded from the curriculum?
Did you like the reading?	What are the blocks to success related to this issue?	How have these events in history been rearranged and expressed, and to whose advantage?
Who benefitted?	What historical narrative is commonly accepted about this topic?	
Which one is correct, A or B?	What is the author's basic point of view?	How could this material help us in our everyday lives?
Where is it located?	What's another point of view on this same story?	How can this information help you succeed?
How many countries are there in Africa? (*"How" question but still closed*)	What is possible?	
	What resonates for you?	Why do you think you never learned this before?
	What if…..?	
Where did it take place?	What do you mean by your statement?	Why hasn't the problem been solved?
On a scale of 1-5, how big is this issue?	Can you tell me more?	
	What does it feel like?	How does it look to you?
	What part is not yet clear?	
	What leads you to think that way?	How has the way you were educated impacted your knowledge of history?
	What do you think is best?	
	What is exciting to you about this?	How do you feel about it?
	What's missing in the story?	
	What….? What else?	How has your perspective and/or behavior changed as a result of your learning?
	What is an example?	

4. Make use of the included activities (a checklist)

While the study guide offers a number of activities to engage the group and help deepen learning, here are a few suggestions on how to make best use of these activities.

> Use the list below as a checklist to prepare for highly effective learning sessions.

1. ☐ **Read the assigned section** and go through the study guide activities to ensure you are knowledgeable enough to lead the group through the study.

2. ☐ **Select the activities** you will use. You may decide to select a few, all or your own.

3. ☐ **Pay attention** to the specific competencies that activities are meant to amplify.

4. ☐ Modify or **adapt the activities** you will use if needed to fit your group. (All of the activities included in the study guide are written for audiences that include high school students or adults).

5. ☐ **Reproduce any materials** you will use as activity worksheets.

6. ☐ Decide if the activity should be done in **one session or more** than one.

7. ☐ **Prepare an outline** for how you will lead the session in an engaging way that deepens learning (doesn't have to be real formal).

8. ☐ If time permits, **locate additional resources** as appropriate to deepen your knowledge of the content. Some suggestions will be listed in each section under "Note to Study Leader."

9. ☐ Remind the group in advance about the topic and how they might prepare.

10. ☐ **Jot down a few questions** that open up the thinking of the study group members. (See sample questions on previous page).

My Reflection: As a facilitator, which of the items above (1-10), come easiest for you? _____Which will you want to work on a bit more? _____ How will you do that? _____

A Sample Session Format (adapt as appropriate)

Get Started	Engage Content	Make Meaning	Wrap Up
Introduction Objectives Excite: Why it matters Starting Questions	Dig Deeper with questions and activities	Summarize meaning of the section Application to real life Reflect on starting and new questions	Next session topic and date

- **Get Started:** Start strong and create simple ways to garner participation, such as: *reading the section made me feel….* or after clarifying the "agenda" for the session (purpose, time, etc.) ask, *in one sentence, what's your initial thought about the reading? Or what questions came to mind?*

- **Engage Content:** To review the content of the section, have someone summarize it briefly (they can use the included Section Snapshot and Main Points), then ask others if there's anything to add to the summary. The group will make meaning of it later, so this is just to get the gist of what the author is saying.

o What initial questions do you have about the reading? Let's brainstorm some.

o Dig into the activities, whichever you select of those in this study guide or alternatives you've created. Facilitate the conversation around the activities.

- **Make Meaning:** The group should address: What meaning was there in the material we just covered? What was most significant? Most challenging? In what ways does it prompt you to function differently? How well did we address our starting questions? Are there any new ones? (Some of these questions are built into the activities.)

Wrap Up: Close the session by summarizing, gathering feedback about the value of the session if you want, and sharing the time/date/logistics for next session.

May the learning journey begin.

II. Study Activities, Worksheets, Handouts

Sankofa bird
It is not wrong to go
back for that which you
have forgotten

Preface: the Matter of Racial Memory
book pages 1-8

Objective	Group members gain clarity about the connection between the study of history, the content of one's memory, and the impact they both have on identity development. Secondly, this is a good place to build familiarity with the west African Adinkra symbols (throughout the book) and the power of symbols in a society.
Snapshot	The preface provides an overview of the construct and purpose of memory for the individual and society, and, in particular Black people's collective *historical* memory.
Main Points	⮝ There are several types of memory.
	⮝ Environmental factors have an influence on memory.
	⮝ The *content* of our education influences what we remember.
	⮝ Black people's loss of memory can be likened to *collective dementia*, which impacts both our psychology and behavior.
	⮝ Studying our history from an historically accurate, African-centered lens can reignite a positive collective historical memory.
Words, People, Places	• Symbols and artifacts (used throughout the book) • Systemic • Memory (direct & indirect) • Identity • Amos Wilson • Paulo Freire

Note to Study Leader

1. Refer to the checklist on page 17 for general preparation of study group session.
2. Gather some basic information of the various forms of memory (short term, long term, sensory, direct, indirect).
3. Research the local school curriculum and identify to what extent African history is offered.
4. Familiarize yourself with the west African Adinkra symbols (which are used throughout the book) and locate an Adinkra symbol chart (many are online, and one is included with activities).

Quotable

"History is far from a dead thing. We carry it within us. We are unconsciously controlled by it in many ways, and history is literally present in all that we do. It could scarcely be otherwise, since it is to history that we owe our frame of reference, our attitude, our identities, our aspirations" --James Baldwin, The White Man's Guilt, 1965

Have the Group Make a List of Opening Questions

1. Before delving deeply into the section, have the group generate a list of starting questions by completing the first section of the Activity #1 worksheet. Creating questions helps the participants own their learning.
2. As the study leader, compile the group's questions, removing any duplicates.
3. Then, at the end of the final activity, lead the "Closing the Session" section which asks you to refer back to the starting questions to help the group determine how well and to what extent the group answered their questions.

Preface, Activity 1: Power of Symbols Worksheet

Competencies: ☑ Critical Thinking ☑ Questioning ☐ Innovation ☑ Collaboration ☑Reflection

My Starting Questions: Before delving into the book's **Preface**, generate a list of starting questions by answering: *When I look at the title and topics of this section of* **Connections Remembered**, *what initial question(s) come to my mind?*

1.

2.

Now, on to Activity #1:

Purpose: to explore the power of symbols and artifacts to affirm a group's identity

We hope you observed the use of African symbols throughout the book. These are Adinkra symbols. They are included to highlight and celebrate African cultural elements. Symbols have power, and they are all around us. This activity helps learners explore the use of symbols and artifacts in their world, which promote a *particular* group's identity and cultural norms.

Instructions:

❶ Individually, conduct a short internet search to discover the role of symbols and artifacts in a culture. Then, in the box below, write your response to: *What power do symbols have in influencing cultural attitudes as well as one's sense of identity?*

❷ There are lots of symbols, and they are everywhere, though we take them for granted. *What are 3-5 prominent symbols in American culture?*

a. Now, compare your list with other participants and explore these questions:

Which are most commonly repeated on the lists?

_____ _____ _____

_____ _____ _____

Where do you see them represented most often?

To what extent (circle below) do you see symbols in America that are positive representations of non-white cultural standards and norms?

Very often | **Often** | **Sometimes** | **Very little** | **Rarely**

As a group, answer: Why or why not?

_____

_____

Reflect: What impact do you think these symbols have had on you?

Preface, Activity 2: Connecting to African Symbols Worksheet

Competencies: ☑ Critical Thinking ☐ Questioning ☐ Innovation ☐ Collaboration ☑ Reflection

Purpose: to explore the Adinkra symbols, which reflect and affirm African culture

Instructions:

❶ Research the origins of the Adinkra symbols.

a. Where did they originate? _____ When? _____

b. How are the Adinkra symbols most often used?

❷ Using an Adinkra chart (a sample chart is on the next page), identify three that you like most and why.

Favorite Adinkra symbols	Why were you drawn to them?
1.	
2.	
3.	

❸ What value might come from increasing use of these symbols and other African artifacts for people of African descent?

Reflect: What can you do in your home or any other spaces you control to add symbols that support positive African/Black cultural identity?

Sample Adinkra Symbols Chart

There are many more charts that include different, with more or less symbols. Some have variations in meaning.

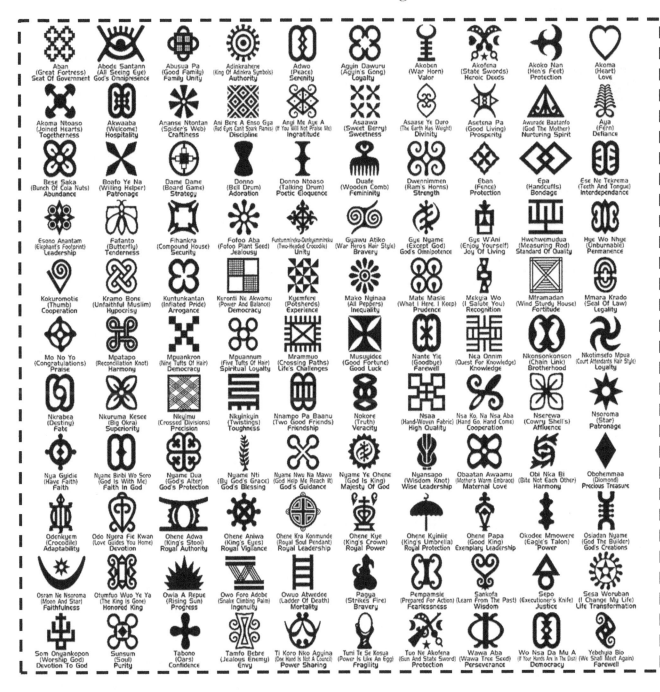

Preface, Activity 3: My Identity Today Worksheet

Competencies: ☑ Critical Thinking ☑ Questioning ☐ Innovation ☑ Collaboration ☐ Reflection

Purpose: to explore personal identity and how it affects our everyday lives

What is Identity? Identity answers "Who Am I? and expresses who you think you are based on: 1) **social identity**—the information society says about who you are, and 2) **personal identity** –characteristics that you believe are significant and convey your level of value individually and as part of a larger group. **Social identity** can influence **personal identity**. Some examples of identity statements refer to race, physical traits, gender, class, economic status, marital status, beliefs/convictions, affiliations, traits, occupation, etc. For example, two people with the same job may not answer *Who Am I?* in the same way if they don't both view their job as key to their identity. One's sense of identity can change over time. And, it is not uncommon for people to say "I don't know who I am."

Instructions:

 ❶ **My Identity:** Use descriptive words to express how you think of yourself when answering, *Who Am I?* using the two types of identity below.

My social identity	My personal identity
(How friends, family, school, job and the larger society describe who you are)	(Characteristics and roles that YOU believe establish your sense of value in life)

a. Now, compare your responses. How consistent is who *society* says you are and who *you* say you are?

☐ **Very consistent**	☐ **Mostly the same**	☐ **Some difference**	☐ **Very different**

b. If very different, how do you account for the difference?

```
┌─────────────────────────────────────────┐
│                                         │
│                                         │
│                                         │
│                                         │
│                                         │
└─────────────────────────────────────────┘
```

c. How did you "learn" that this is who you are? (people, experiences, etc.)

```
┌─────────────────────────────────────────┐
│                                         │
│                                         │
│                                         │
│                                         │
└─────────────────────────────────────────┘
```

d. With the group, spend some time sharing the responses to any or all of the items above.

Make note of what you found most interesting when listening to others share their responses? _____

_____

Identity Interview Worksheet

(you need two copies of the worksheet)

❷ **Conduct an Interview:** Identify two people at least 10 years older than you are to learn how their sense of personal identity may have changed over time because of life experience. Use these three questions to conduct the interviews. (If possible, record the interviews.)

Interviewee's Name:_____ **Approximate age:**_____

Question	Response
a. How would you explain who you are today? *(for example: characteristics, roles, sense of self, racial sense, important traits that make you who you are)*	
b. Would that be the same description you would have given 10-15 years ago?	
c. What experiences helped change (or if it hasn't changed, use the word "shape") how you view yourself?	

d. From the interview, what two things stuck out most for you?

_____   _____

 Sharing: Once the interviews are complete, be prepared to: a) Share what you learned from the interviews with a partner, and b) Engage in a conversation with the entire group, gathering key insights from the activity.

Reflect: How might these identity activities help you think about your personal identity going forward?

Preface, Activity 4: Memory in Your Family Worksheet

Competencies: ☐ Critical Thinking ☐ Questioning ☑ Innovation ☑ Collaboration ☑ Reflection

Purpose: to remember and reflect on family history and traditions

> **Memory and the Family:** In the preface of **Connections Remembered**, there are references to different types of memory. One of the ideas about memory, which has an impact on how identity is formed, is **vicarious** memory. This activity looks at vicarious memory (related to your family) which includes oral traditions and stories shared with you that you were not present to experience. Yet they influence you.

❶ What are two oral traditions your parents or grandparents passed down to you, such as family stories, sayings, or traditions? (Examples: *Do your best and the best will come back to you, you can't trust anybody, your grandfather didn't take no stuff down south, we dress up to go shopping etc.*)

Family saying, tradition or story	
Family saying, tradition or story	

What effect, if any, do you think these stories, etc. have had on how you think and behave?

❷ With the entire group, be ready to share and write your saying, tradition and legend on labeled flip chart/board so the entire group can see them all. Then select someone's saying that speaks to your life today and share why.

❸ Reflect on this quote and share what it says to you, especially related to family history.

"History is far from a dead thing. We carry it within us. We are unconsciously controlled by it in many ways, and history is literally present in all that we do. It could scarcely be otherwise, since it is to history that we owe our frame of reference, our attitude, our identities, our aspirations" -James Baldwin

❹ Finally, create your own *saying* that you would share with the next generation as a key to navigating their world. Write it here.

Closing the Section (for study leader)

Activity four was the last activity for the *Preface, The Matter of Racial Memory*. Before moving to the next section, have the group reflect on the key ideas and take a moment to review the group's opening questions for this section.

You might ask: *How well did the group answer the questions? Are there any other thoughts regarding those questions? Is there anything going forward that individuals or the group should explore related to the topics covered?*

Now, provide the group time to think about any new questions related to this section. Record them below for possibly deepening the learning at a later time.

Our New Questions about…. Symbols and Artifacts, Identity, Memory

1.

2.

Section 1: A Framework for Studying African History book pages 13-34

Objective	Group members are reminded of the value of studying African history, including establishing deeper connections with self, community and the world. They will also enhance their awareness and analysis related to "who" is telling the history and "why."
Snapshot	Section 1 establishes a framework for studying history and other disciplines. It shares several ways that studying history adds value to the individual and a group's life. It makes clear that there are nearly always political reasons for "how" history is told. Finally, the section explores two competing models of history. One is centered in a white supremacist Eurocentric worldview, and the more ancient one, is the Afrocentric model, which was supplanted to reinforce white superiority and Black inferiority.
Main Points	⏶ There are many good reasons to study history, among them is history's influence on every other academic discipline.
	⏶ African people have a continuous history of great accomplishment, and that history began millions of years before the slave trade.
	⏶ History is never an objective reality; the facts are told from *someone's* worldview.
	⏶ There are two competing and distinctly different models of history, and students of history should be aware of both.
	⏶ African history has been deliberately removed from textbooks, which has adversely impacted Black identity.

Words, People, Places	• Afrocentric (ancient) history
	• Eurocentric (revised) history
	• Worldview
	• W.E.B. DuBois
	• Amos Wilson

Note to Study Leader	1. Refer to the checklist on page 17 for general preparation of study group sessions.
	2. Note that Activity 1 has tasks that cover more than one session, with items 3 and 4 being addressed in a follow-up session.
	3. Use digital and print resources to learn more about the term "Afrocentrism."

Quotable	*Would it not be wise for American [Blacks] themselves to read a few books and do a little thinking for themselves? It is not that I would persuade [Blacks] to become communists, capitalists, or holy rollers, but whatever belief they reach, let it for God's sake be a matter of reason and not of ignorance.* –W. E. B. DuBois, cited on pg. 17 of **Connections Remembered**

Make a List of Opening Questions

1. Before delving deeply into the section, have the group generate a list of starting questions by completing the first section of the Activity #1 worksheet. Creating questions helps the participants own their learning.

2. As the study leader, compile the group's questions, removing any duplicates.

3. Then, at the end of the final activity, lead the "Closing the Session" section which asks you to refer back to the starting questions to help the group determine how well and to what extent the group answered their questions.

Section 1, Activity 1: Know Your People Worksheet

Competencies: ☐ Critical Thinking ☑ Questioning ☐ Innovation ☑ Collaboration ☑ Reflection

My Starting Questions: Before delving into **Section 1** of the book, generate a list of starting questions by answering: *When I look at the title and topics of this section of* **Connections Remembered**, *what initial question(s) come to my mind?*

1.

2.

Now, on to Activity #1: *(which will require two sessions)*

Purpose: to explore one's personal family lineage and key highlights

Instructions:

❶ Individually, use the worksheet on page 36 to record the names of as many family members as you can in 10 minutes. Begin with those around your same age; then go to your parents' and their parents' siblings, etc. Finally, list those younger than you.

❷ In small groups, compare your lists, and talk through these two questions:

a. What and who are you glad you remembered?

Who did you discover you *don't* know among your family members? *(For example: I realized I never knew my great grandparents or my mother's oldest brother)*

❸ Before the next session, contact one relative either in your generation or older to see how many more names you can fill in. Ask them to identify one significant story or event related to two of the older relatives.

Story/Event:
Story/Event:

❹ Upon return to the session, hold a conversation about what you learned and why you think it matters to know your personal history.

 **Reflect:** What do you feel is the impact on you of knowing your family lineage?

Activity #1 Worksheet: My Personal History

My grandparents' relatives (as far back as you can go)	My parents' immediate relatives (Your aunts and uncles, grandparents)	My generation (Your brothers and sisters, cousins, etc.)	Younger than me (nieces, nephews, great nieces, 2nd cousins, etc. not in your generation)

Section 1, Activity 2: What Do You Know? Black History Worksheet

Competencies: ☐ Critical Thinking ☐ Questioning ☐ Innovation ☑ Collaboration ☑ Reflection

Purpose: to explore your personal placement in history

Instructions:

❶ On the lines below, list 5 or more historical events (or people) in the Black experience **in America** that took place _before_ your birth.

_____   _____
_____   _____
_____   _____
_____   _____

❷ On the lines below, list 5 or more historical events (or people) in the Black experience in **America** that took place _during_ your lifetime.

_____   _____
_____   _____
_____   _____
_____   _____

❸ Now list 5 or more events or significant people in **African** history BEFORE Black people were brought to America in human bondage.

_____   _____
_____   _____
_____   _____
_____   _____

❹ Compare your lists with others and share what you have in common and why you chose the events you chose.

Notes:

Reflect: What in your home or educational experience impacted how much you know or don't know about Black history?

Section 1, Activity 3: Value of History Worksheet

Competencies: ☑ Critical Thinking ☑ Questioning ☐ Innovation ☑ Collaboration ☑ Reflection

Purpose: to recall and reflect on the value of studying one's own history

Instructions:

❶ Review Section 1 of **Connections Remembered**, *Africa, A Framework for the Study*, and respond to the following questions to help you recall the key ideas.

a. What are two of the five reasons given for the importance of studying history? Talk with your group to provide examples that support these reasons.

Why study history?	Example showing "why" important
1.	
2.	

b. When students are provided textbooks, as discussed on page 22 of **Connections Remembered**, what are two questions (your own or from the section) that would help them critically analyze the content?

_____

_____

c. What are the two competing models of history? Then in small groups, talk about how each might affect Black people's sense of pride and healthy identity.

Model _____	Model _____
Impact(s):	Impact(s):

❷ As a group, identify five Black history authors whose writings help elevate the achievements of Black people.

_____   _____

_____   _____

_____   _____

 Reflect: Place a checkmark (✓) by any of these authors the group identified above whose books were included in your education. Then respond to: Why do you think they were included and the others were not included?

Closing the Section (for study leader)

Activity three was the last activity for the *Section 1, Africa, A Framework for the Study*. Before moving to the next section, have the group reflect on the key ideas and take a moment to review the group's opening questions for this section.

You might ask: *How well did the group answer the questions? Are there any other thoughts regarding those questions? Is there anything going forward that individuals or the group should explore related to the topics covered?*

Now, provide the group time to think about any new questions related to this section. Record them below for possibly deepening the learning at a later time.

Our New Questions about.... Africa, A Framework for the Study

1.

2.

Section 2: Africa, A Magnificent Land and its Geography book pages 35-53

Objective	Group members will increase knowledge of the historical attacks and misrepresentations about the physical size, attributes and richness of the African continent. Participants will also increase geography fluency and appreciation for Africa—as a way to enhance healthy identity and placement.
Snapshot	The content of this section centers around the location and physical size of Africa in comparison with the of the world's land masses. It highlights Africa's geographical features such as waterways, mountain ranges, diverse land types, and the abundant, highly sought-after natural resources. Finally, the most current list of the many countries of Africa and dates of their independence from European colonialist nations are included.
Main Points	⌃ Africa is a CONTINENT, not a country!
	⌃ Eurocentric politics and map-making led to misrepresenting the size of Africa (to diminish it) and Europe (to elevate its stature).
	⌃ Africa is a very large and geographically diverse land mass that includes more countries than any other continent in the world.
	⌃ Africa was the focal point of a late 19th Century ruthless European power grab that destroyed the existing African nation's boundaries.
	⌃ African nations liberated themselves politically from European colonizers, most did so during the second half of the 20th Century.

Words, People, Places	• Continent
	• Peters Projection Map
	• Cartography
	• Topography
	• Partition of Africa

Note to Study Leader

1. Refer to the checklist on page 17 for general preparation of study group sessions.
2. Look up Peters Projection map so you have basic familiarity with it.
3. Review a map that shows the islands that are part of Africa (some are not shown on page 49 of the book); see "Answer Key" on page 106 for such a map so that you are aware of the locations of all six island/nations.

Quotable

We seek to no longer be victimized by others as to our place in the center of world history. We do this not because of arrogance but because it is necessary to place Africa at the center of our existential reality, else we will remain detached, isolated and spiritually lonely people. –Molefi K. Asante (cited on pg. 35 of ***Connections Remembered***.)

Make a List of Opening Questions

1. Before delving deeply into the section, have the group generate a list of starting questions by completing the first section of the Activity #1 worksheet. Creating questions helps the participants own their learning.
2. As the study leader, compile the group's questions, removing any duplicates.
3. Then, at the end of the final activity, lead the "Closing the Session" section which asks you to refer back to the starting questions to help the group determine how well and to what extent the group answered their questions.

Section 2, Activity 1: Check Out Africa's Geography Worksheet

Competencies: This activity is meant to enhance recall of basic knowledge.

My Starting Questions: Before delving into **Section 2** of the book, generate a list of starting questions by answering: *When I look at the title and topics of this section of* **Connections Remembered**, *what initial question(s) come to my mind?*

1. _____

2. _____

Now, on to Activity #1:

 Instructions: ❶ Either individually or in teams, answer these 10 basic questions to show how much you know about places and words related to Africa's geography.

1. Peters projection map is…	
2. How many African countries are there?	
3. What are two of Africa's prominent mountain ranges?	
4. Name five of Africa's abundant natural resources.	
5. Africa is about how many square miles… and the only continent that is larger is…	_____ sq miles _____ largest
6. Cartography is the practice of….	
7. The Earth's surface is made up of mostly…	a. mountains b. water c. land
8. What are three waterways that surround Africa?	
9. Name three prominent lakes in Africa.	
10. What are the names of three islands that are a part of the African continent?	

 Reflect: What value do you see in having some basic knowledge of the geography of Africa?

Section 2, Activity 2: Liberating African Nations Worksheet

Competencies: ☑ Critical Thinking ☐ Questioning ☑ Innovation ☑ Collaboration ☑ Reflection

Purpose: to increase knowledge of Africa's 20ᵗʰ Century political independence

Instructions:

❶ The greatest number of African countries to break free of white colonialism did so in 1960. How many were there? _____ List six of those countries that are in the western part of Africa.

_____   _____   _____

_____   _____   _____

Select two of the countries in Africa that declared their independence since 1975. Conduct a bit of research to cite one factor that led to their independence.

Country....	Broke from...	Factor

❷ While the African independence timeline indicates South Africa became independent in 1910, you are probably familiar with Nelson Mandela playing a key role in liberating South Africa in 1994. Conduct some research to learn why these "freedom" dates (1910 and 1994) are different, then answer a, b, and c below.

a. Who gained control in 1910? _____ From? _____

b. What historic role did Nelson Mandela hold before his death?

c. How would you describe the quality of life for Black South Africans prior to "freedom" in 1994?

❸ Within small groups, share your responses to a, b and c above. Then, as small groups, come up with three ideas on:

a. The similarities between Black people's condition in the U.S. today and the responses the group identified for answer c.

1.
2.
3.

b. What can Black people do today to become more "independent" from the racist system in America?

1.
2.
3.

A large group report out will follow the small group work.

Reflect: What role can you play, large or small, to help Black people achieve freedom from oppression in everyday life?

Section 2, Activity 3: African Map Savvy Worksheet

Competencies: ☑ Critical Thinking ☐ Questioning ☐ Innovation ☑ Collaboration ☑ Reflection

Purpose: to build familiarity with the changing geography of Africa

Africa has been under assault for a long time, and the maps of Africa, over time, reflect that relentless assault on Africa. The resources of Africa and the advanced culture and accomplishments caused great envy among European and Asian nations alike. Africa has never been able to rest from this assault as its resources continue to be exploited to create wealth throughout the world.

Instructions:

❶ *How map savvy are you?* Complete as much of the map of Africa's countries (on page 53 of **Connections Remembered** as possible in 15 minutes. See how much you know, then commit to add two more each week.

❷ Compare the two maps of African nations (on the next two pages) before the slave trade and during the colonial era (1881-1914), with the map of Africa today (See **Connections Remembered**, page 49). What observations can you make when comparing the maps?

❸ Talk in groups about these observations. Note below a few observations from others that you had not considered.

Reflect: How might being knowledgeable of Africa's geography help you understand the challenge of Africans gaining cultural and economic control today?

Two Maps

African Empires Prior to 1500 CE

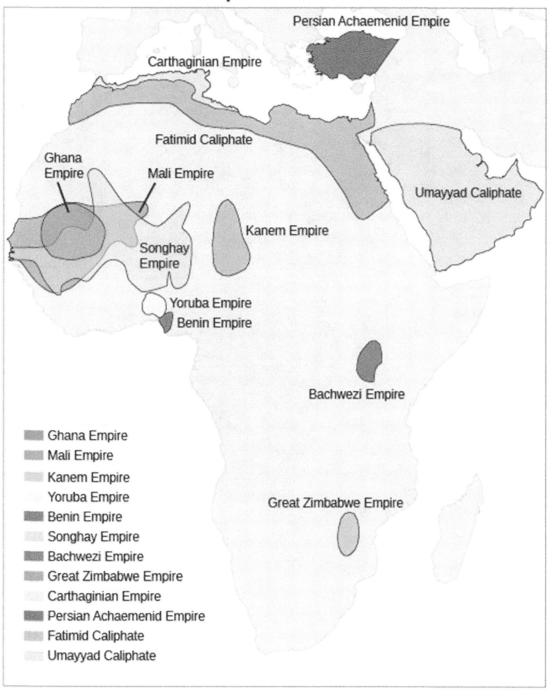

Spanish
French
French
Spanish
French West Africa
British
Portuguese
British
Free
British
German
Spanish
French
British
French
Italian
British
British
British
Italian
French
Italian
Free
British
German
Belgium
Atlantic
Ocean
Portuguese
British
Portuguese
German
British
British
British
German
Indian
Ocean
French
British

African Colonies after the Berlin Conference of 1884

Closing the Section (for study leader)

Activity three was the last activity for the *Section 2, Africa, A Magnificent Land and its Geography*. Before moving to the next section, have the group reflect on the key ideas and take a moment to review the group's opening questions for this section.

You might ask: *How well did the group answer the questions? Are there any other thoughts regarding those questions? Is there anything going forward that individuals or the group should explore related to the topics covered?*

Now, provide the group time to think about any new questions related to this section. Record them below for possibly deepening the learning at a later time.

 **Our New Questions about....** Africa, A Magnificent Land and its Geography

1.

2.

Section 3: Africa and the Origins of Life
book pages 54-71

Objective	Group members will build basic knowledge of two rarely addressed aspects of ancient African history. The first is that Africa was the center of the Earth's first single land mass before the continents were separate land masses as they are today. The second is that even before the emergence of the first human life, Africa was home to the world's first biological life. These historical occurrences provide a sense of grounding and rootedness for people of African descent.
Snapshot	This section addresses the geological and archaeological phenomena related to the origins of the Earth and its physical structure. Scientists confirm that the Earth began as a single land mass called Pangaea with Africa at its center. Over millions of years, Pangaea split into two separate land masses, called Laurasia and Gondwanaland. The study of the shifting Earth provides a literalness to the saying, "Africa, center of the world."
	This section continues by showing how this composition set the stage for early life forms to begin, then move out from Africa to the rest of the world.
Main Points	⅄ The Earth is believed to have begun billions of years ago with Africa at its center.
	⅄ Scientists describe ancient Earth's land mass as a single supercontinent called Pangaea, which later split into two supercontinents.

⅄The southern supercontinent, Gondwanaland, with Africa at its center, enabled the earliest biological life to spread throughout the world.

⅄The ancient history of the shifting Earth is key to reconnecting people of African descent to a very long historical narrative.

Words, People, Places	• Pangaea • Panthalassa • Gondwanaland • Laurasia • Continental fit • Continental drift
Note to Study Leader	1. Refer to the checklist on page 17 for general preparation of study group sessions. 2. For Activity 1: The study leader can make this a five-minute team competition, or each person can answer the multiple-choice questions, then the group talk through the answers. Advise participants not to focus on individual scores; the point is to have a fun way to internalize these history facts. (See "Answer Key" on page 107 of this study guide).

Quotable *History is the landmark by which we are directed into the true course of life. The history of a movement, the history of a nation, the history of a race is the guidepost of that movement's destiny, that nation's destiny, that race's destiny.*

—Marcus M. Garvey

Make a List of Opening Questions

1. Before delving deeply into the section, have the group generate a list of starting questions by completing the first section of the Activity #1 worksheet. Creating questions helps the participants own their learning.

2. As the study leader, compile the group's questions, removing any duplicates.

3. Then, at the end of the final activity, lead the "Closing the Session" section which asks you to refer back to the starting questions to help the group determine how well and to what extent the group answered their questions.

Section 3, Activity 1: The Facts of African Origins, Worksheet

Competencies: This is an information recall activity, which builds a foundation for deeper learning.

My Starting Questions: Before delving into **Section 3** of the book, generate a list of starting questions by answering: *When I look at the title and topics of this section of* **Connections Remembered***, what initial question(s) come to my mind?*

1. _____

2. _____

Now, on to Activity #1:

Purpose: to enhance knowledge of the basic facts about the African origins of life

 Instructions: Take five minutes to answer these 8 multiple-choice questions. The study leader will have the group members share their answers to collectively recall, confirm and talk about these 8 "facts."

1. How old do you guess the Earth is, based on scientists' theory?	a. 4.4 trillion years b. 3.6 billion years c. 1.2 million years d. 4.5 billion years
2. Scientists used fossils to learn life began in Africa. What is a fossil?	a. The hardened remains of an animal, human or plant preserved in the Earth's crust. b. A sample of material for everyday use. c. An object from the past found in water.
3. The oldest single-celled life form was discovered in:	a. Swaziland b. Tanzania c. Sierra Leone d. Egypt
4. The theory of the continents being all connected is called _____ meaning "all lands."	a. Laurasia b. Pangaea c. Panthalassa d. Gondwanaland
5. The southern supercontinent from which life spread was called:	a. Laurasia b. South America c. Gondwanaland d. Australia
6. The term used to describe when all the Earth's water was unified as one:	a. Pangaea b. Panthalassa c. Ocean d. International Waters
7. Along with Africa, which of the following was a part of the southern supercontinent, from which earliest life spread.	a. Russia b. South America c. China d. Canada
8. Scientists tell us the Earth's crust sits atop of several slab-like sections, which are called:	a. Land bridges b. tectonic plates c. continuous continents

Great job!

Section 3, Activity 2: Historical Placement Worksheet

Competencies: ☑ Critical Thinking ☐ Questioning ☑ Innovation ☑ Collaboration ☑ Reflection

Purpose: to think about how historical viewpoints impact groups of people

Section 3 takes us back to the very beginning of life on Earth. It helps situate Black people in history, starting with our homeland, the continent of Africa.

Instructions:

Group Activity: In a group, read aloud and discuss the following quote about the purpose of history. Talk together to answer the four questions below that help make meaning of the quote.

"History should tell a people who they are, where they came from and what their potential is as a people. If it fails to do so, it is useless." [3]

Questions	Our Main Responses
1. How has the history to which you have been exposed accomplished or not accomplished the ideas in the quote?	
2. How does this section of the book connect to the quote?	
3. What are some ways, in today's society, you see Black history being highlighted, made a priority, or celebrated?	
4. How else can Black history be elevated to inspire and encourage Black people to have pride in our Black heritage?	

Reflect: What 1-2 things can you do to make African/Black history more meaningful and empowering personally?

---

[3] Browder, A. *Nile Valley contributions to civilization*, p. 30

Section 3, Activity 3: Black Scientists Worksheet

Competencies: ☑ Critical Thinking ☐ Questioning ☐ Innovation ☑ Collaboration ☑ Reflection

Purpose: to explore misconceptions about and representation of Blacks in science

The scientists credited for much of the research in Section 3 related to African origins are Caucasian. There are many reasons, some rooted in racism, why this is the case. Yet, the world's first scientists were Africans, and they were key to developing the world's first civilizations. This activity asks participants to explore Black people in the sciences.

Instructions: ❶ Conduct a short internet search (10-20 minutes) to identify and list the names of five (5) prominent Black scientists and their accomplishments.

Black scientist	One Achievement
1.	
2.	
3.	
4.	
5.	

❷ Use a wall chart to combine participants' lists to create a longer list of accomplished Black scientists. How many different ones did the group come up with?

❸ In small groups, decide which of these scientists' innovations impact your everyday life the most. How? List a few of them below.

_____

_____

_____

Reflect: Which scientist would you want to learn more about as a result of these conversations? Why?

Section 3, Activity 4: Black Exploitation Through Science

Competencies: ☐ Critical Thinking ☐ Questioning ☑ Innovation ☑ Collaboration ☑ Reflection

Purpose: to explore how white scientists' experiments have exploited Black people

Instructions: ❶ There have been cases where white scientists have exploited Black people for profit and "advancement." Look up and examine two of the four situations below that subjected Black people to scientists' inhumane experiments.

Situation/Experiment	When?	Two key points about it
Henrietta Lacks		
Tuskegee Syphilis Experiment		
The Bell Curve		
James Marion Sims, gynecology studies		
Other?		

❷ Compare your notes with the group. How did these examples make you feel? What stuck out most for you?

_____

_____

_____

❸ In small groups, brainstorm and agree on three ideas that teachers, mentors and parents can use to encourage Black students to become more curious about various science fields.

1. _____
2. _____
3. _____

Reflect: How have you been influenced by the negative attitudes displayed towards Black people by the scientific community, if at all?

Closing the Section (for study leader)

Activity four was the last activity for the *Section 3, Africa, And the Origins of Life*. Before moving to the next section, have the group reflect on the key ideas and take a moment to review the group's opening questions for this section.

You might ask: *How well did the group answer the questions? Are there any other thoughts regarding those questions? Is there anything going forward that individuals or the group should explore related to the topics covered?*

Now, provide the group time to think about any new questions related to this section. Record them below for possibly deepening the learning at a later time.

Our New Questions about…. Africa, and the Origins of Life

1.

2.

Section 4: Africa and the Origins of Humanity
book pages 72-90

Objective	Group members will examine the scientific evidence collected over the last 150 years which validates that human beings first emerged in Africa and subsequently migrated "out of Africa" into the rest of the world.
Snapshot	Section four focuses on the science-based "out of Africa" model of human origins. It documents the explorations of scientists, beginning in the 19th century, and their search for evidence that pinpoints the location where human beings first emerged. The section also points out the unrelenting efforts made by white scientists to refute the African origins of humanity and that Africa is the mythological "Garden of Eden."
Main Points	⌃ The historic efforts by whites to diminish the value of Africa in the emergence of humanity have been discredited by researchers over the last 100 years.
	⌃ A major reason for the effort to diminish the role of Africa in human origins was to provide a justification for the African slave trade and its subsequent brutal racist system of chattel slavery.
	⌃ The Piltdown forgery and Coonian thesis were two major attempts to undermine the "out of Africa" model of human beginnings.
	⌃ Africa is the mythological "Garden of Eden" inhabited by people who practiced social cooperation.

Words, People, Places	• Out of Africa model of history • Multi-regional model of history • Louis and Mary Leakey • Charles Darwin • Africa's Great Lakes region • Olduvai Gorge • Lake Turkana • Omo Ethiopia • Klasies River South Africa
Note to Study Leader	1. Refer to the checklist on page 17 for general preparation of study group sessions. 2. Look up a bit of information about the Out of Africa model of ancient humanity's spread. 3. Be sure to have either flip chart(s) or wall charts for posting responses in Activity 2, #3. 4. See "Answer Key" for Activity 4 on page 107.
Quotable	*"Black young people must know the historical truth that Africa was the epicenter of human origins – the mythological "Garden of Eden." These statements are not wishful thinking; they are grounded in the facts of Africa's history. Africa is where the first humans emerged and where the earliest civilizations were spawned." –pg. 87 of* **Connections Remembered**

Make a List of Opening Questions

1. Before delving deeply into the section, have the group generate a list of starting questions by completing the first section of the Activity #1 worksheet. Creating questions helps the participants own their learning.

2. As the study leader, compile the group's questions, removing any duplicates.

3. Then, at the end of the final activity, lead the "Closing the Session" section which asks you to refer back to the starting questions to help the group determine how well and to what extent the group answered their questions.

Section 4, Activity 1: Beliefs About Human Origins Worksheet

Competencies: ☑ Critical Thinking ☑ Questioning ☐ Innovation ☑ Collaboration ☑ Reflection

My Starting Questions: Before delving into **Section 4** of the book, generate a list of starting questions by answering: *When I look at the title and topics of this section of* **Connections Remembered***, what initial question(s) come to my mind?*

1.

2.

Now, on to Activity #1:

Purpose: to examine beliefs fostered by society about the world's first humans

Instructions: ❶ Your beliefs (prior to you having read Section 4).

a. Describe what your beliefs were, if any, about the location of the first humans.

b. Where did these beliefs come from?

c. If you didn't have any beliefs about the location of human origins, what impact might this have had on your perspective about yourself and the world?

❷ After reading Section 4, the group will engage in interviewing each other about beliefs about human origins and what is similar and dissimilar. Use the guide on the next page.

Rotating Interviews: Interview two participants about their beliefs related to humanity's origins. Spend 10 minutes asking each other the four questions below. Record your responses in the spaces provided.

Questions	Interview #1	Interview #2
a. What ideas did you learn about where humankind began?		
b. How did the ideas you had about human origins affect your concept of Africa?		
c. If the "out of Africa" concept was not covered during your schooling, why do you think that was the case?		
d. Growing up, did anyone in the family demonstrate their pride in Africa's history? If so, who and how?		

❸ After the rotating interviews, the facilitator will lead the group in sharing any observations they gathered that would impact Black students' feelings about their history. Be ready to share your notes from the chart above.

 Reflect: How do you think knowledge of human origins affects identity development?

Section 4, Activity 2: "Deception, Deception" Worksheet

Competencies: ☑ Critical Thinking ☐ Questioning ☐ Innovation ☑ Collaboration ☑ Reflection

Purpose: to explore the efforts to deny Africa as the place of human beginnings

Instructions: ❶ In small groups, discuss these three questions:

1. What purpose did the Piltdown forgery and Coonian Thesis serve?
   _____
   _____
   _____

2. Describe the "out of Africa" model and the "Multi-regional" model of human origins. Write your notes here. (The group will debrief to ensure understanding of the two ideas.)

Out of Africa model of human spread	Multi-regional model of human spread

3. **Deception and Racism Today:** What are two deceptive beliefs or myths promoted by American society to undermine the history and accomplishments of Black people?
   1) _____
   2) _____

❷ **Debrief:** Join the group in reviewing responses to #2 and 3. Then **post** responses to #3 on a flip or wall chart. Be ready to join the group conversation, that will use these questions: *Which did you already know about? Which are new to you? What are your thoughts about the <u>truth</u> of the items posted (related to responses to #3 above)?*

Reflect: From your perspective, what was the most important idea in Section 4, and why?

Section 4, Activity 3: Human Origins, Teach Back

Competencies: ☑ Critical Thinking ☐ Questioning ☐ Innovation ☑ Collaboration ☑ Reflection

Purpose: to analyze and teach each other key ideas on the theories of human origins

Instructions: ❶ **Teach Back Activity:** Divide into three groups. Cut the three questions below into individual slips of paper and give one to each group. Each small group should spend about 20-30 minutes together to answer the assigned questions. Be advised that the teams will be the "teachers" of the topic they are covering and will have 5-7 minutes to teach the group about their conclusions and support for those conclusions.

✂ --

a. What reason(s) could there have been to promote the "multi-regional" model of humanity' spread across the world over the "out of Africa" model? Be ready to spend 5-7 minutes to teach the entire group about your conclusions and how you support those conclusions.

✂ --

b. Who was Carleton Coon, and how has Carleton Coon's Thesis been perpetuated and reinforced in society especially during and since the Civil Rights Movement? Be ready to spend 5-7 minutes to teach the entire group about your conclusions and how you support those conclusions.

✂ --

c. What evidence does ***Connections Remembered*** share that indicates early humans had a *sharing culture*? Now compare and contrast that way of life with U.S. culture today. Create an "Ancient Africa" versus "U.S. Today" chart. Be ready to spend 5-7 minutes to teach the group about your conclusions and how you support those conclusions.

✂ --

❷ **Group Reflection:** In the full group, have a conversation about: What was most significant about what you heard in the teach-back activity? Who can you share this information with, and how might they benefit from hearing it?

Section 4, Activity 4: First Humans "Facts" Worksheet

Competencies: This is an information recall activity, which builds a foundation for deeper learning.

Purpose: to recall and retain some key facts about human origins

 Instructions: ❶ Take five minutes, either in teams or as individuals, to answer these 5 multiple-choice questions. The group will share their answers to the 5 "facts."

1.	How many years ago is it believed that humans began moving out of Africa to the rest of the world?	a. 40,000 b. 130,000 c. 2 million
2.	What is one of the popular stories about humanity beginning in Europe or Asia, rather than Africa?	a. Genesis Creation Story b. Piltdown Man Story c. Cherokee Creation Story
3.	After 100 years of trying to dispute Darwin's claim of human origins in Africa, finally a properly dated fossil was found. Which describes it?	a. Cro-Magnon man, France, 1868 b. East African man in Tanzania, 1959 c. Java Man, Indonesia, 1898
4.	A famous family who played a role in finding many fossils validating the African origin of humanity.	a. Leakeys b. Coonians c. Rockefellers
5.	Name three locations in Africa where the earliest human fossils were discovered.	a. Tanzania, Ethiopia, South Africa b. Egypt, Iran and Angola c. Senegal, Guinea and Kenya

❷ **SEQUENCING ACTIVITY**: Humans emerged and developed in Africa over millions of years. Place the following in sequential order of their emergence (oldest to newest) and fill in the other columns. ***Homo sapiens, Homo erectus, Australopithecus, Homo sapiens sapiens, Homo habilis***

Sequence (oldest to newest fossils)	One characteristic	Approx. age (exact unknown)
1.		
2.		
3.		
4.		
5.		

Closing the Section (for study leader)

Activity four was the last activity for the *Section 4, Africa, And the Origins of Humanity.* Before moving to the next section, have the group reflect on the key ideas and take a moment to review the group's opening questions for this section.

You might ask: *How well did the group answer the questions? Are there any other thoughts regarding those questions? Is there anything going forward that individuals or the group should explore related to the topics covered?*

Now, provide the group time to think about any new questions related to this section. Record them below for possibly deepening the learning at a later time.

Our New Questions about…. Africa, and the Origins of Humanity

1.

2.

Section 5: The Nile Valley Origins of Civilization

book pages 91-110

Objective	Group members will analyze and make judgments about the historical evidence refuting the Eurocentric de-Africanizing of Egypt. This is accomplished by delving into the research done by a number of recognized historians that clearly points to an African origins of civilization, beginning in the Nile Valley.
Snapshot	Up until the 19th Century it was commonly accepted by historians that Greek civilization (the first recognized civilization in Europe) had its origins in Africa, specifically Kemet (Egypt).
	Beginning in the 19th Century, as a justification for the enslavement of Africans and plantation slavery, white historians began a dramatic *reimagining* of Africa and African people. These reconceptualizations purported to prove that Africa has always been a backwards uncivilized continent populated by savages.
	This historical reimagining conflicted with the prior understanding asserted by the Greeks themselves that their civilization was the result of their education in Africa with the people of Kemet.

Main

Points

⌃ The Nile Valley, south of Kemet (Egypt), was the location of the world's earliest civilizations.

⌃ The populating of Kemet was the result of a *south to north* migration of Africans along the Nile River .

⌃ The people of early Kemet self-identified as Black and asserted that their origins were from southern migrants (Nubians).

Words, People, Places	• Bruce Williams
	• Chancellor Williams
	• Martin Bernal
	• Dr. Josef Ben-Jochannan
	• Nile Valley
	• Nubia
	• Kemet
	• Ta-Seti

Note to Study Leader	1. Refer to the checklist the on page 17 for general preparation of study group sessions.
	2. Research efforts made to "de-Africanize" Egypt.
	3. For Activity 3, locate a World History textbook (or two) and analyze the information included about Egypt and the world's first civilization.
	4. See "Answer Key" for Activity 4 on page 107.

Quotable	*"The de-Africanizing of Egypt was no simple reimagining of history – it was part of the white western world's aggressive campaign to grow its global power and influence. The Eurocentric model was a foundational element for achieving that objective. Recreating the flow and interpretation of historical events is a privilege of the powerful."* Pg. 94-95 of **Connections Remembered**

Make a List of Opening Questions

1. Before delving deeply into the section, have the group generate a list of starting questions by completing the first section of the Activity #1 worksheet. Creating questions helps the participants own their learning.

2. As the study leader, compile the group's questions, removing any duplicates.

3. Then, at the end of the final activity, lead the "Closing the Session" section which asks you to refer back to the starting questions to help the group determine how well and to what extent the group answered their questions.

Section 5, Activity 1: Nubia's Greatness Worksheet

Competencies: ☑ Critical Thinking ☑ Questioning ☑ Innovation ☑ Collaboration ☑ Reflection

My Starting Questions: Before delving into **Section 5** of the book, generate a list of starting questions by answering: *When I look at the title and topics of this section of* **Connections Remembered**, *what initial question(s) come to my mind?*

1. _____

2. _____

Now, on to Activity #1:

Purpose: to reflect on the importance of the discovery of ancient Nubia

Instructions: ❶ Using Section 5 and other resources, describe the Nile Valley, its location, special characteristics, and importance to early civilizations.

What is it?	
Where?	
Characteristics…	
Why important?	

❷ What do you now understand is important about studying Nubia that you didn't know before and why? _____

_____

❸ Section 5 introduces the world's very first civilizations. Look at the descriptions of "civilization" in Section 5, then look up two other definitions of "civilization." Record your responses in the spaces below.

Definition #1	
Definition #2	

❹ Now, with the group, share those definitions and how they support or deny the existence of Africa's first civilizations. Record any observations you make from the group conversation.

_____

_____

❺ Finally, work together to come up with an agreed-upon team definition of "civilization."

We believe *civilization is....* _____

_____

Reflect: How do you think conducting your own research and thinking with others to create your own definition builds individual skills?

Section 5, Activity 2: History of Anti-Blackness Worksheet

Competencies: ☑ Critical Thinking ☐ Questioning ☑ Innovation ☑ Collaboration ☑ Reflection

Purpose: to explore the politics of race and history

Instructions: ❶ The effort to de-Blacken Egypt was another way of reinforcing negative stereotypes about Blackness. What are some of the myths/stereotypes about "Blackness" you hear in your environment?

_____

_____

_____

_____

❷ Conduct an internet search on *"Black racial stereotypes"* and discuss what you found with the group and the possible social purposes for these stereotypes.

_____

_____

_____

_____

_____

❸ Describe the conditions and reasoning behind the effort of white historians to deAfricanize Kemet (Egypt). With the group, draw conclusions about what their efforts were meant to accomplish. Record in the space below.

_____

_____

_____

_____

Reflect: What impact does it have on you to be a part of a group that has had negative things said and believed about the group for several hundred years?

Section 5, Activity 3: Textbooks & the Nile Valley Project Sheet

Competencies: ☑ Critical Thinking ☑ Questioning ☐ Innovation ☑ Collaboration ☑ Reflection

Purpose: to evaluate history textbooks and their role in perpetuating Eurocentric views about the world's first civilizations

Instructions: ❶ **Team Project:** In teams of 2 or 3, evaluate two high school World History textbooks' section on the world's first civilization by completing the chart below. (Either bring a hard copy of the textbooks or download World History textbooks in PDF format for use).

	Textbook_____ Year published_____	Textbook _____ Year published _____
1. What does it say about the very first civilization?		
2. How is Egypt portrayed in regard to ethnicity/race?		
3. Is Egypt (Kemet) viewed as a part of Africa or in another way?		
4. What else did you observe about how the textbooks address the first civilizations?		

❷ The study group facilitator will have four flip charts, one labeled for each of the questions. Your team should be ready to post the team's answers. Teams will then walk around and review the flip chart information.

With the entire group, be ready to respond to the question: What do the responses have in common and what's different? _____

_____

❸ With the group, share thoughts on: How does the group think these textbooks might affect how students think about themselves and their world? (There are no right answers).

```


```

❹ If you have to choose one book or neither, which would you choose and why or, if neither, why not? _____

_____

 **Reflect:** Thinking now about the textbooks you used in school, what were some key messages to you about your identity as a Black person?

Section 5, Activity 4: Recalling the Facts Worksheet

Competencies: This is an information recall activity, which builds a foundation for deeper learning.

Purpose: to recall and retain some key facts about the first civilizations

 Instructions: Fill in or choose the correct "facts" about Nubia.

1. In relation to Egypt, Nubia was ….	__north __east __south __west
2. When did it become a priority for whites to de-Africanize Egypt?	_____
3. The Nile River flows through how many of today's African countries?	How many?_____ Name five.
4. Nubia had pharaohs before Egypt.	___ True __False
5. The Nile, before joining to become one river, has two parts. They are called…	_____ and _____
6. What name did the Egyptians use to self-identify?	a. Asian-African b. Kemmiu c. Mesopotamians
7. Three of the accomplishments of ancient Nubia noted in the book are….	_____ _____ _____
8. How many Nile cataracts are there?	a. two b. nine c. six
9. "Ethiopia" was a termed used by the Greeks to describe the people in East Africa and the word is translated to mean…	_____
10. We may never know the full story of Nubia because…	a. Key archaeological sites are no longer accessible b. Europeans don't want us to know c. History classes do not teach about it d. All of the above e. None of the above

Closing the Section (for study leader)

Activity four was the last activity for the *Section 5, The Nile Valley Origins of Civilization.* Before moving to the next section, have the group reflect on the key ideas and take a moment to review the group's opening questions for this section.

You might ask: *How well did the group answer the questions? Are there any other thoughts regarding those questions? Is there anything going forward that individuals or the group should explore related to the topics covered?*

Now, provide the group time to think about any new questions related to this section. Record them below for possibly deepening the learning at a later time.

Our New Questions about.... The Nile Valley Origins of Civilization

1.

2.

Section 6: Egypt's Contributions to World Civilization book pages 111-133

Objective	Group members will uncover the historical evidence verifying that the inhabitants of the Nile Valley were the creators of the earliest human civilizations. Readers will gain knowledge to support the assertion that Europe's ancient Greek civilization was the "daughter" of Africa.
Snapshot	Section 6 first examines the relationship that existed between Africa and the European country of Greece and how the Greeks were intellectually enriched through their involvement with Africans.
	This section shares evidence that the major center of learning in the ancient world was the African Mystery System, centered in the Nile Valley.
	Finally, the section makes clear that the Judeo-Christian faith (and others) is based upon writings from the African Mystery System.
Main Points	⅄ In the Nile Valley, life was conceived of as a continuing spiritual quest.
	⅄ The earliest rulers of Kemet (Egypt) were Nubian conquerors who came from the region known today as Sudan.
	⅄ The religious writings for Judeo-Christian beliefs were largely influenced by the spiritual writings from the Pyramid Texts.
	⅄ The spectacular architecture built during the Old Kingdom of Kemet was the product of students who studied in the African Mystery System.

Words, **People,** **Places**	• Step Pyramid • Great Pyramid • Pyramid Texts • Maat • John Jackson • Gerald Massey • Godfrey Higgins • Anthony Browder • Dr. Josef Ben-Jochannan
Note to **Study** **Leader**	1. Refer to the checklist on page 17 for general preparation of study group sessions. 2. Related to Activity #1, refresh or review some of the contributions ancient Egyptians made to civilization. 3. Have flip chart or white board for Activity 2. 4. See "Answer Key" for Activity 4 on page 107.
Quotable	*"It was through rigorous study in the Mystery System that the major Greek philosophers and mathematicians gained their knowledge. Socrates, Plato, Pythagoras, Thales, Heraclitus, and others all studied in the temples of Kemet, receiving instruction about the Mystery System, which was the foundation of ancient civilization. Europe has proclaimed the roots of its civilization harken back to the ideas of the major Greek philosophers. If that is the case, Europe owes much to the Africans who were their instructors, guides, and exemplars."* p. 129 of ***Connections Remembered***

Make a List of Opening Questions

1. Before delving deeply into the section, have the group generate a list of starting questions by completing the first section of the Activity #1 worksheet. Creating questions helps the participants own their learning.

2. As the study leader, compile the group's questions, removing any duplicates.

3. Then, at the end of the final activity, lead the "Closing the Session" section which asks you to refer back to the starting questions to help the group determine how well and to what extent the group answered their questions.

Section 6, Activity 1: Egyptians as Innovators Worksheet

Competencies: ☑ Critical Thinking ☑ Questioning ☐ Innovation ☑ Collaboration ☑ Reflection

My Starting Questions: Before delving into **Section 6** of the book, generate a list of starting questions by answering: *When I look at the title and topics of this section of* **Connections Remembered***, what initial question(s) come to my mind?*

1. _____

2. _____

Now, on to Activity #1:

Purpose: to honor and celebrate the advanced achievements of Africa's Egyptians

The historically documented achievements of the ancient Black Egyptians still have an impact today. They began using their scientific, mathematical, moral/ethical, and artistic knowledge as early as 4,000 b.c., and many still marvel at those accomplishments.

Instructions:

❶ In the top boxes of the chart on the next page, write any four major contributions Egyptians made to early civilization (from Section 6, Page 92 of **Connections Remembered** or use your own research).

❷ In the bottom boxes, for each one, think about and write how each of those contributions may still be having an impact today.

❸ Next, compare what you wrote in the boxes with group members. Determine what you have in common, while expanding your thinking about the lasting impact of your African ancestors' ingenuity.

Contribution	Contribution	Contribution	Contribution
Impact Today	**Impact Today**	**Impact Today**	**Impact Today**

 Reflect: Think about this: We are all making history right now that will impact the next generations. How do you hope to impact the future?

Section 6, Activity 2: Egyptians, Religious Influence Worksheet

Competencies: ☐ Critical Thinking ☐ Questioning ☐ Innovation ☑ Collaboration ☑ Reflection

Purpose: to examine the impact ancient Egypt had on the world's major religions

Instructions: ❶ Where (country or area) do people typically believe the major Christian beliefs originated? _____

❷ Define the following terms related to religion:

Monotheistic _____

Polytheistic _____

Anthropomorphism _____

❸ In a group, discuss and debate: *What are some examples of how the writings in the ancient Pyramid Texts, especially those in the "Book of Wise Instruction," later became a part of Judeo-Christian beliefs?* Record your notes, along with the group, on a flip chart or white board.

❹ Think about and record similarities among the ancient ideas of the Holy Trinity.

Holy Trinity of Nubia 3300 b.c.	Holy Trinity of Kemet 2300 b.c.	Holy Trinity of Christianity 20-30 ad.

 Reflect: How difficult was it for you to think and talk about the source of Christian belief? And why?

Section 6, Activity 3: Egyptians, Advanced Education Worksheet

Competencies: ☑ Critical Thinking ☐ Questioning ☑ Innovation ☑ Collaboration ☑ Reflection

Purpose: to recall and make meaning of the African Mystery System today

Instructions: ❶ Provide a *brief* overview of the curriculum of the Mystery System (see book pages 127-129 and anything else you find related to it).

Overview:

How were the Greeks involved with it? _____

_____

❷Thinking of today's world, if you were developing a high school core curriculum to enhance 21st Century skills and knowledge, what would you keep, take away, and add from the Mystery System curriculum?

Keep	Take Away	Add

❸ In groups, compare each person's *keep, take away and add* items from your chart above. Have everyone explain why they selected these things and how this makes the curriculum stronger for today's students.

❹ **Group Reflection:** What do you think about the advanced education in Africa thousands of years ago compared to how Black children are educated today?

Section 6, Activity 4: Remembering the Pharaohs Worksheet

Competencies: This is an information recall activity, which builds a foundation for deeper learning.

Purpose: to recall the powerful building projects of the Black Pharaohs of Egypt

 Instructions: ❶ Take the 10-question quiz to dig into the powerful leadership and accomplishments of Egyptian/Nubian pharaohs. Share responses with the group.

1.	Some of the greatest building projects were done during Egypt's Old Kingdom, which was also called…	a. The Pyramid Age b. The Bronze society c. The Greek renaissance
2.	Three of the greatest pharaohs that led Egypt's great building projects were:	a. Nefertari, Netcher, and Imhotep b. Unas, Pythagoras, and Homer c. Zoser, Khufu, and Khafre
3.	Which pyramid was called the world's first skyscraper?	_____
4.	The pyramid that is one of the seven wonders of the world….	_____
5.	The three major pyramids of the Giza complex are….	a. Small ones outside of Egypt b. Great Pyramid, Pyramid of Khafre and Pyramid of Menkaure c. The Sphinx, Luxor, and Aswan
6.	There are also pyramids outside of Egypt. Name two places.	_____ _____
7.	Another astonishing architectural accomplishment of the Black pharaohs was a structure built from a single stone. What was it?	_____
8.	There are how many sphinxes of all sizes along a single road in Egypt?	a. 500 b. 75 c. 1300
9.	The designer of the Step Pyramid was a multi-talented architect named…	_____
10.	The oldest existing religious writings were found in the pyramids and are called…	a. The holy scriptures b. The Pyramid Texts c. The hymn of Horus

Great job! The achievements of the ancient Black pharaohs still reverberate today.

Closing the Section (for study leader)

Activity four was the last activity for the *Section 6, Egypt's Contributions to World Civilization.* Before moving to the next section, have the group reflect on the key ideas and take a moment to review the group's opening questions for this section.

You might ask: *How well did the group answer the questions? Are there any other thoughts regarding those questions? Is there anything going forward that individuals or the group should explore related to the topics covered?*

Now, provide the group time to think about any new questions related to this section. Record them below for possibly deepening the learning at a later time.

Our New Questions about.... Egypt's Contributions to World Civilization

1.

2.

Section 7: Other Major African Civilizations *Before* the Rise of Europe book pages 134-153

Objective	Group members will build foundational knowledge of West Africa's history and the political forces that set the stage for Europe's violent rise and rape of Africa, including the devastating transatlantic slave trade.
Snapshot	Section seven amplifies the genius of Africans throughout the continent, with an emphasis on the advanced civilizations that began in western Africa. The section is meant to be a bridge *from* the unrivaled ancient Nubian and Egyptian civilizations developed without western influence *to* the dismal 400+ years of Black oppression today. The section concentrates on the sophisticated, ancient west African civilizations. Among them were the Moors, Ghana, Mali and Songhai. These vibrant cultures stood in sharp contrast to the European Dark Ages, setting the stage for European envy and their drive to conquer these resource-rich cultures.
Main Points	⅄ The cultures and civilizations begun in Nubia and Egypt spread throughout the continent of Africa, then eventually the world.
	⅄ Resource-rich West Africa benefited from and enhanced some of the contributions from Nubia and Egypt before the Europeans arrived.
	⅄ The Black African Moors took their skills to southwest Europe, and advanced culture and civilization.
	⅄ Ghana, Mali, and Songhai are the most renowned of the West African Golden Age empires during the middle ages.

⅄ There were many more advanced cultures in West Africa before the Europeans arrived and ravaged Africa.

Words, People, Places	• Moors • Sahara Desert • Rivers: Senegal, Gambia, Niger, Volta • Lake Chad • Iberian Peninsula • Timbuktu • Mansa Sundiata • Mansa Musa • Sonni Ali
Note to Study Leader	1. Refer to the checklist on page 17 for general preparation of study group sessions. 2. See "Answer Key" for Activity 1 on page 107. 3. Study the included maps of the West African empires in comparison to Africa's countries today to be able to identify where they are located today. 4. Select one of the authors who writes about the Golden Age of West Africa and do a bit of background reading.
Quotable	"*Nothing in Africa had any European influence before 332 B.C. If you have 10,000 years behind you before you even saw a European, then who gave you the idea that he moved from the ice-age, came all the way into Africa and built a great civilization and disappeared, when he had not built a shoe for himself or a house with a window?*" -Dr. John H. Clarke, quoted in ***Connections Remembered,*** Pg. 134

Make a List of Opening Questions

1. Before delving deeply into the section, have the group generate a list of starting questions by completing the first section of the Activity #1 worksheet. Creating questions helps the participants own their learning.

2. As the study leader, compile the group's questions, removing any duplicates.

3. Then, at the end of the final activity, lead the "Closing the Session" section which asks you to refer back to the starting questions to help the group determine how well and to what extent the group answered their questions.

Section 7, Activity 1: West Africa is Golden Worksheet

Competencies: ☑ Critical Thinking ☑ Questioning ☐ Innovation ☑ Collaboration ☑ Reflection

My Starting Questions: Before delving into **Section 7** of the book, generate a list of starting questions by answering: *When I look at the title and topics of this section of* **Connections Remembered**, *what initial question(s) come to my mind?*

1. _____

2. _____

Now, on to Activity #1:

Purpose: to explore the facts and contributions of ancient West Africa

Instructions:

❶ What do you think the authors' intentions were in writing sections 7 and 8, the closing sections of the book? How does section 7 connect with the previous sections of the book?

I believe the author's intentions were…	
The connection I see to the earlier parts of the book	

❷ Compare responses with the other group members. Summarize your conclusions.

❸ To recall key points, answer the following questions in teams of three.

1. What were the major three empires of West Africa's Golden Age?	
2. Name two of the Golden Age of West Africa leaders.	_____
3. Which religion began to dominate and influence ancient west Africa?	_____
4. Culture and civilization are believed to have come to west Africa from…	a. The Nile Valley b. Eastern Europe c. Istanbul, Turkey
5. Two lesser known and smaller west African kingdoms were…	_____ _____
6. The desert in Africa that was a connector for exchange is called…	_____
7. One part of Europe enjoyed the benefits of ancient west Africa. That area was…	a. Iberian Peninsula b. Bosnia c. Paris, France
8. The Moors were from northwest Africa, and "Moor" means….	_____

Great job recalling characteristics of West Africa's Golden Age!

Section 7, Activity 2: Locating the Empires Worksheet

Competencies: This is an information recall activity, which builds a foundation for deeper learning.

Instructions: ❶ To pinpoint the locations of the ancient empires, review the maps in Section 7 (*Connections Remembered,* pages 144-149). Now, draw the empires of Ghana, Mali and Songhai on this modern map. (There will be some overlap of empires.)

❷ Other questions to ponder:

a. Why is the Ghana of the Golden Age not located in today's country called Ghana?

b. How would you describe the conditions in most of Europe during Africa's Golden Age?

c. List 3-4 pieces of information in Section 7 that are most memorable for you.

Section 7, Activity 3: How West Africa Rose Worksheet

Competencies: ☑ Critical Thinking ☐ Questioning ☑ Innovation ☑ Collaboration ☑ Reflection

Purpose: to explore and make assumptions about the factors leading to the rise of ancient West Africa

Many factors were at play that led to the rise of the great west African kingdoms and empires. We may never know all of them. As we think about civilizations, communities, even organizations that rise, it might be informative to explore the possible factors that enabled West Africa to rise to great heights.

Instructions: ❶ **Team project:** Think about the Kwanza principle, Kujichagulia (self-determination). Go online and look up the word to learn more about what it means.

❷ After reading Section 7, think about factors that played a part in ancient west Africans creating great, self-determining empires (You can add or delete any categories below you feel necessary).

Factors	When thinking about the West African Empires, how did these factors help them become self-determining?
Economics	
Natural resources	
Government system	
Attitude/psychology	
Cultural pride	
Education	

❸**Prepare**: Each team will present their conclusions on a flip chart, slide show, etc. to the group.

❹Within your group, identify the factors Black people need to better develop in order to achieve Kujichagulia as business owners, communities, etc.

_____

_____

_____

_____

 **Reflect:** What do you suggest as one step, even a small one, to help Black people advance to a higher level in business, community and schools?

Section 7, Activity 4: My West African People Worksheet

Competencies: ☐ Critical Thinking ☐ Questioning ☐ Innovation ☑ Collaboration ☑ Reflection

Purpose: to investigate and imagine one's own connections to west African nations

Instructions: ❶ Assume, as history tells us, that the majority of Black people in the Americas descended from west African peoples, (i.e., our forebears were enslaved and brought to America during chattel slavery). Respond to the following.

a. What information do you have that helps you connect to your roots in west Africa? You can also ask family members who have done DNA or other genealogy tests.

b. What else might you do to help get a better idea about your west African identity?

c. If you were to visit a west African country (this is becoming a very popular travel destination for African Americans), how would you use anything you learned in Section 7 to prepare for your visit? What else would you want to know before going?

❷ With the entire group: 1) Share your responses to the items above, and 2) answer: *In what ways, if any, does knowledge of west Africa influence how you see your identity today?*

Reflect: How do you feel, knowing your ancestors were powerful nation builders when you compare that with the state of Black people today?

Closing the Section (for study leader)

Activity four was the last activity for the *Section 7, Other Major African Civilizations before the Rise of Europe*. Before moving to the next section, have the group reflect on the key ideas and take a moment to review the group's opening questions for this section.

You might ask: *How well did the group answer the questions? Are there any other thoughts regarding those questions? Is there anything going forward that individuals or the group should explore related to the topics covered?*

Now, provide the group time to think about any new questions related to this section. Record them below for possibly deepening the learning at a later time.

Our New Questions about.... Other Major African Civilizations *before* the Rise of Europe

1.

2.

Section 8: Europe's Violent Rise in Africa
book pages 154-174

Objective	Group members will build or sharpen knowledge and perspective on the historical events and practices that precipitated the rise of European power and the ideology of white supremacy.
Snapshot	Section eight continues to build a historical bridge between African people's great, self-determining societies to what seems an enduring second-class status and denigration across the world, premised on a white declaration of Black inferiority established in tandem with the transatlantic slave trade.

The section achieves its points by examining: 1) the European Dark Ages as a major impetus for the raid on Africa, 2) the European wealth building derived from control of Africa including the transatlantic slave trade and European colonialism, and 3) the Berlin Conference and the 20th Century Partition of Africa. All of these have a threaded message of white superiority and Black inferiority. |
| **Main Points** | ⋏ Europe was enmeshed in its Dark Ages as west African civilizations were flourishing and under attack by marauders.

⋏ Campaigns into west Africa for human slave trading began with the Portuguese.

⋏ Millions of West Africans were dispersed, mostly throughout the Americas through the brutal slave trade, with a massive loss of life.

⋏ A declaration of Black inferiority was fabricated by white "academics" and religious leaders to justify the enslavement of African people. |

⋏ A process to lead Africans to feel "less than human" was put in place to help make the slave system more effective.

⋏ The Berlin Conference and later Partition of Africa laid an enduring foundation for building white wealth on Black backs.

Words, People, Places	• European Dark Ages • Genocide • "Seasoning" process • Colonization • Berlin Conference • Partition of Africa
Note to Study Leader	1. Refer to the checklist on page 17 for general preparation of study group sessions. 2. Activity 1 may require two sessions. 3. See "Answer Key" for Activity 3 on page 107.

Quotable	*"We are artificial 'nations' carved out at the Berlin Conference in 1884, and today we are struggling to build these nations into stable units of human society…we are in danger of becoming the most Balkanized continent of the world.* -- Julius K. Nyerere, Tanzania's President (1964-1985)

Make a List of Opening Questions

1. Before delving deeply into the section, have the group generate a list of starting questions by completing the first section of the Activity #1 worksheet. Creating questions helps the participants own their learning.

2. As the study leader, compile the group's questions, removing any duplicates.

3. Then, at the end of the final activity, lead the "Closing the Session" section which asks you to refer back to the starting questions to help the group determine how well and to what extent the group answered their questions.

Section 8, Activity 1: European Tactics Handout

Competencies: ☑ Critical Thinking ☑ Questioning ☐ Innovation ☑ Collaboration ☑ Reflection

My Starting Questions: Before delving into **Section 8** of the book, generate a list of starting questions by answering: *When I look at the title and topics of this section of* **Connections Remembered***, what initial question(s) come to my mind?*

1. _____

2. _____

Now, on to Activity #1:

Purpose: to think about some of the tragic European tactics used to conquer and steal the resources of West Africa

Note: This activity will require time to prepare and then to present, so it may require two sessions.

Instructions: ❶ Print out and cut the graphic on the next page into the six squares. Break into small teams and provide each team with one of the squares (some squares may be leftover if there are not enough teams.)

❷ Each team will prepare to present their topic, guided by: *This is one of the tragic tactics Europeans used to conquer West Africa and diminish Africans' self- identity.*

Each team should review Section 8 to gather basic information about their topic, then do online research to gather more detail. The team should decide "how" they want to present their topic (visuals, videos, activity, etc.) Each team should be sure they cover: What, When, Where, How, and the Effect.

The Middle Passage	Making a slave: The Seasoning Process
The Berlin Conference	Neo-colonialism
Colonialism	The church and the educational system

❸ **Team Reports**: Each team has up to 8 minutes to share their knowledge of the tactic they studied. After all teams have presented, ask the group to respond to the following:

a. Which of these traumatic tactics affected you the most? Why?

b. What else would you want to know about either of these tactics?

 Reflect: Are there any tactics today that demonstrate the same kind of vicious attempts to subjugate a group of people? Explain.

Section 8, Activity 2: Liberating Africa Worksheet

Competencies: ☑ Critical Thinking ☐ Questioning ☐ Innovation ☑ Collaboration ☑ Reflection

Purpose: to delve into the backgrounds and accomplishments of Africa's post-colonial first presidents

Instructions: ❶ Select and research one of the many "first" African presidents during Africa's middle-20th century independence movement. Learn how they sought to reestablish a renewed, healthy African identity and gain political and economic control over their homeland.

1. *President's Name (pick one)* ☐**Kenneth Kaunda** ☐**Jomo Kenyatta** ☐**Patrice Lumumba**
2. ☐**Somora Machel** ☐**Kwame Nkrumah** ☐**Julius Nyerere** ☐**Sekou Touré**

3. *What did he do, where and when?*	
4. *Successes…*	
5. *General biography (optional: have a photo to show)*	
6. *Challenges and betrayals…*	
7. *Anything else?*	

❷ Next, form groups based on the leader selected (*for example, everyone choosing Jomo Kenyatta will be in the same group*). Compare notes and ideas to create one presentation. Each group will choose how they will share the story of their "first" African president.

❸ What traits do you think distinguished these individuals as leaders?

_____

_____

Note: *Some examples of leadership traits: courage, commitment, delegation, resilience, empathy, inspirational, confidence, decision-making skills, accountability, knowledge, integrity, communication, planning/strategic, passion/drive, etc.*

Reflect: What are your strongest leadership traits now? Which would you like to develop? And how can you use them to address situations of oppression or discrimination?

Section 8, Activity 3: My People Are Everywhere Worksheet

Competencies: This is an information recall activity, which builds a foundation for deeper learning.

Purpose: to reflect on the many locations African people were dispersed during the enslavement of African people

Instructions:

❶ Review Section 8 and use online research if needed, to respond to the following questions to help identify where our captured ancestors were taken:

1. Define the word "diaspora." _____

_____

2. Recall the names of **four** main coastal regions from which Africans were taken into slavery. _____ _____

_____ _____

3. Name **three** of the places where the largest number of Africans were taken into slavery.

_____ _____ _____

4. The **four** major (there were others too) European nations that raped Africa of its resources and enslaved African people were: _____

_____ _____ _____

❷ On the map on the next page, label or mark the following places:

- The various continents depicted on the map

- Three main West African ports

- Two major slave ports in the U.S.

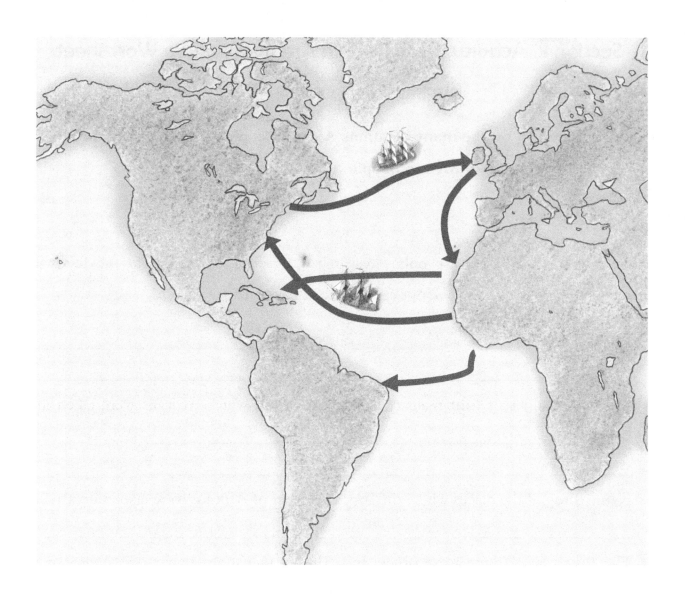

 **Reflect**: After studying this book, to what extent do you feel a greater kinship with Black people from different parts of the world? Explain.

Section 8, Activity 4: Seasoning Process: Impact Today Worksheet

Competencies: ☑ Critical Thinking ☐ Questioning ☑ Innovation ☑ Collaboration ☐ Reflection

Purpose: to draw parallels between systems for **"keeping slaves in their place"** during chattel slavery and today

Instructions: ❶ Review the five goals of the plantation seasoning process "To Make Them Stand in Fear" in Section 8, on page 168. Also, if available, review chapter 4 of Kenneth Stampp's book, *Peculiar Institution* (It is titled <u>To Make Them Stand in Fear</u>). How do you see any or all of these goals still being reinforced today?

Goal	How is it reinforced today?
1. Establish and maintain strict discipline	
2. Implant in the bondsmen themselves a consciousness of personal inferiority…	
3. Awe them with a sense of their master's enormous power	
4. Persuade them to take an interest in the master's enterprise and to accept his standards of good conduct	
5. Impress upon the bondsmen their helplessness, to create in them *"a habit of perfect dependence"* upon their masters.	

❷Share answers in the group; compare responses and make note of new insights.

_____

_____

❸**Resistance:** Now, follow-up that conversation by listing below at least one way (for each goal) YOU can resist these "slave making" activities designed to create a slave mindset. (These numbers should correspond with the numbers in the chart on the previous page.)

    1.

    2.

    3.

    4.

    5.

Section 8, Activity 5: Diaspora Connections Worksheet

Competencies: ☑ Critical Thinking ☐ Questioning ☑ Innovation ☑ Collaboration ☑ Reflection

Purpose: to understand and strengthen "kinship" among Diasporan Africans

Instructions: ❶ You will use interviewing to connect with an adult west African living in the U.S. (someone who came or whose parents came to the U.S. any time since 1970). The aim is to gather their feelings and thoughts about the relatedness between African Americans and themselves.

Name: _____ Age group:_____

1. What country do you call your home in Africa? _____ If there is a national group/clan within that country to which you belong, what is it called? _____

2. What did you learn about your relationship with Africa's descendants in the United States and the Caribbean?

3. What can you share about the role and involvement of your home country in the transport of Africans to America during the slave trade? _____ _____

4. How would you describe your sense of kinship and connection to Africans in America?

5. What do you think are the major influences for your belief about this kinship?

6. What else would you like me to know about your African national group?

[ ]

7. How can we improve the sense of connection between us?

[ ]

❷ Share your interview findings along with the rest of the group. What did you learn that you didn't know before? _____

_____

- -

❸ **To expand your knowledge**: Have you read any books of fiction by west African authors? Y__ No___ If so, list one or two. _____

_____

If not, maybe you'd like to enhance your connection by reading a book about the African experience in or with America and the interchange of cultural beliefs. Here are a few popular examples:

- **Things Fall Apart**, Chinua Achebe, 1958
- **No Longer at Ease**, Chinua Achebe, 1960
- **Americana**, Chimamanda Ngozi Adiche, 2013
- **Purple Hibiscus**, Chimamanda Ngozi Adiche, 2003
- **Homegoing**, Yaa Ngazi, 2016
- **Behold the Dreamers**, Mbolo Mbue, 2017
- **Other suggestion**: _____

 Reflect: In what ways can you strengthen your identification with Africa and deepen your African Diasporan "kinships"?

Closing the Section (for study leader)

Activity five was the last activity for the *Section 8, Europe's Violent Rise in Africa.* Now, have the group reflect on the key ideas and take a moment to review the group's opening questions for this section.

You might ask: *How well did the group answer the questions? Are there any other thoughts regarding those questions? Is there anything going forward that individuals or the group should explore related to the topics covered?*

Now, provide the group time to think about any new questions related to this section. Record them below for possibly deepening the learning at a later time.

Our New Questions about.... Europe's Violent Rise in Africa

1.

2.

Closing

West African Adinkra symbol, the Sankofa bird
It is not wrong to go back for that which you have
forgotten

The journey to self-discovery, healthy identity, and transformational action is ongoing. Hopefully, this study has encouraged or reinforced your personal quest to know thyself and help succeeding generations of Black young people discover the tremendous power that lies within them. This power arises from the seeds planted when Africa dawned millions of years ago.

Sondai and Lindiwe

Appendix

Activity Answer Keys for Recalling Facts

Most of the activities ask participants to think about and make meaning of the historical material presented in **Connections Remembered**. In some cases, to help participants retain some of the basic what, when and where of key historical points, recall questions are included. What follows are the "*correct*" responses to the recall activities indicated below. (The word "Correct" is italicized because scientific knowledge continues to change.)

Section 2: Activity 1, pg. 43

Answer Key: 1. Map that tries to present the "actual" size of the Earth's land masses 2. 54; 3. Kenya, Kilimanjaro, Ruwenzori Range, Atlas, Drakensberg; 4. See list on page book page 47 for a sampling; 5. 11.7 million, Asia; 6. Map making; 7. B water (71%) ; 8. Atlantic Ocean,, Mediterranean Sea, Red Sea, Indian Ocean; 9.See book page 44 for a number of Africa's lakes ; 10. Cape Verde, Comoros, Madasgasgar, Mauritius, Sao Tome & Principe, Seychelles

Section 2 supplement: a map that displays all of Africa's islands

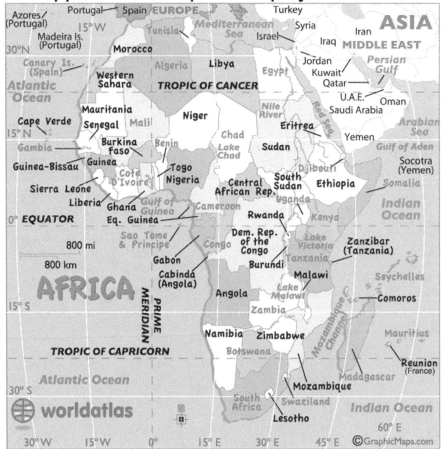

Section 2: Activity 2, pg. 44

Answer Key: 1. 17, list six and independence since 1975 (See book pages 50-51); Responses to answers 2 and 3 should be based on participants research and the study leader researching the information. In #3, four groups of white British clans that dominated South Africa became an independent nation from Britain.

Section 3: Activity 1, pg. 52

Answer Key: 1. D. 4.5 billion; 2. A "hardened remains..."; 3. A Swaziland; 4. B Pangaea; 5. C Gondwanaland; 6. B archaelogy; 7. D 13.8 Billion; 8.BPanthalassa ; 9. B South America; 10. Tectonic plates

Section 4: Activity 4, pg. 63

Answer Key: 1. B, 130,000 years ago; 2. B, Piltdown Man; 3. B, East African...; 4. a, Leakeys; 5. A, Tanzania.....

Sequencing: Australopithecus approx. 4 Million, homo habilis (crude tools); 1.75-2 million, homo erectus (fully upright spine); 1.5 million; homo sapiens (modern humans), between half million – 130,000 years ago; homo sapiens sapiens (more sophisticated humans) 100-200 thousand years

Section 5: Activity 4, pg. 72

Answer Key: 1. South; 2. 19th Century; 3. 11, list on page 98 of the book; 4. True (though lesser known in history) 5. Blue Nile and White Nile; 6. Gondwanaland; 6. B Kemmiu; 7. Choose from items related to: building projects, government systems, agriculture, religious systems, manufacturing, high culture, etc.; 8.c. six; 9. "burnt faces"; 10. D. all of the above

Section 6: Activity 4, pg. 80

Answer Key: 1. A Pyramid Age; 2. C Zoser, Khufu and Khafre 3. Step Pyramid; 4. Great Pyramid; 5. B. Great Pyramid, Khafre and Menkaure (p. 123); 6. The Sudan, Peru, Mexico, Guatamela. 7. The Sphinx (p. 125); 8.C 1300 (p. 127) ; 9. Imhotep; 10. B Pyramid Texts

Section 7: Activity 1 (Item 3), pg. 85

Answer Key: 1. Ghana, Mali, Songhai; 2. Kaya Maghan, Mansa Sundiata, Mansa Musa, Sonni Ali; Askia the Great 3. Islam; 4. A Nile Valley; 5. There are many including Hausa States, Wolof, Kanem Bornu, Oyo, Benin, Ashanti, Yoruba; 6. Sahara; 7. A Iberian Peninsula; 8.Black

Section 8: Activity 3 (Item 1), pg. 97

Answer Key: 1. Dispersion or scattering of a population; 2. There are several including: Senegambia, Sierra Leone, Windward Coast, Gold Coast, Bight of Benin, Bight of Biafra, West Central Africa; 3. See page 161 (largest numbers believed to have been places such as [not in order]: Spanish Carribean Mainland, Cuba, Jamaica, SE Brazil, Bahia, etc.), 4. Portugal, Spain, , France, and England

About the Authors

Sondai and Lindiwe Lester have spent more than 35 years each in public sector leadership. Their vocation has been as liberation theologians at the Pan-African Orthodox Christian Church, followed by service in nonprofit leadership and human development consulting. All along, we have been researching, writing and teaching African and African American history to adults and youth. A source of great pride has been the mentoring relationships we have built across generations of young adults helping them develop their grounding in a strong, healthy racial identity.

For us, historical study is more than a nice pursuit. It is the foundation for tapping into our inner strength as a people to face and be a part of transforming the world. Black history has provided a framework and basis to explain the "why" of our past and current Black condition. It is part of the connective tissue that enabled Black folks' resilience and ingenuity down through the years, despite unthinkable oppression.

We raised our children and supported many families and friends through conversations about race, justice, and personal power. We hope we have planted seeds that continue growing the capacity of our people for self-determination and liberation. We know what *tribe* we belong to; we place it first, and we view the world through the prism of the implications for our tribe's empowerment and well-being.

Sondai has a Master of Arts in Reading, underwent doctoral studies in educational administration and attended seminary at Atlanta's Interdenominational Theological Center. He is President of P.S.E. Institute (Planting Seeds of Excellence) a consultancy for educational development and publishing. Lindiwe has Master of Education (in instructional design) and Educational Specialist degrees. She also is a certified executive coach and facilitator. Lindiwe retired as a nonprofit executive and is currently President of Tap In Coaching and Consulting.

Contact P.S.E. Institute for further conversations, additional books, seminars, educator development, etc.

info@pseinstitutebooks.com, www.pseinstitutebooks.com